Woodlands.explo

For inquiries contact us at <u>mul.den@yahoo.com</u>

HIKING TRAILS

South Kaibab Trail to Cedar Ridge

Enjoy this 2.5 miles (4.5-km) out-and-back trail near Grand Canyon, Arizona. Generally considered a moderately challenging route, it takes an average of 1 h 58 min to complete. This is a very popular area for hiking, so you'll likely encounter other people while exploring. The best times to visit this trail are April through November.

Waypoints

1

Cedar Point

1.5-mile mark

36.0640631, -112.0894046

2

Ooh Aah Point

36.06149, -112.08698

If you want maximum views for minimum effort in the Grand Canyon, the hike on the South Kaibab Trail to Cedar Ridge is about as good as it gets. This route is an awesome option if you want one hike that's doable for most skill levels, has great views, but isn't long or strenuous. The views are remarkable and you don't need to work too hard for them.

The South Kaibab Trail to Cedar Ridge shows off the Grand Canyon from the South Rim, which is where most visitors to the canyon go. It's the second most popular trail in the canyon after Bright Angel Trail, but thanks to its standard 10% gradient, it's a bit easier to complete. While it's enough to get your legs working a bit, it's not narrow or exposed.

To access the trailhead, you must take a shuttle in. There is not parking next to the trailhead because the parking lot is very small. From the trailhead you cascade down several steep switchbacks and continue on until you reach Ooh Ah point. Ooh Ah point is a great place for a wide or panoramic picture and is a fantastic rest spot. Continuing on from Ooh Ah point, Cedar Ridge is only about a half-mile farther down and another 330 feet, and well worth the effort. For one, Cedar Ridge has restrooms. But in addition, Cedar Ridge is a very large flat area where there is room for people to be spread out and not be on top of each other like the trail. Hikers wishing to go further can continue on to reach Skeleton Point and eventually the bottom of the Grand Canyon.

This trail can be extremely hot during the summer so it is imperative that you bring water. Hiking here during the spring months is ideal due to the weather still being very cool. This hike is also very deceiving because you can hike down a while and not feel tired and then realize you have to hike back up. The hike back up is very strenuous and steep and requires way more time than the hike down, so be aware. There may be mules on this trail packing out trash from Phantom Ranch. Should you come up to mules, listen to the handler's directions on how to pass them. If you come up from behind, just announce yourself and listen for instructions on how to pass once it's safe to do so.

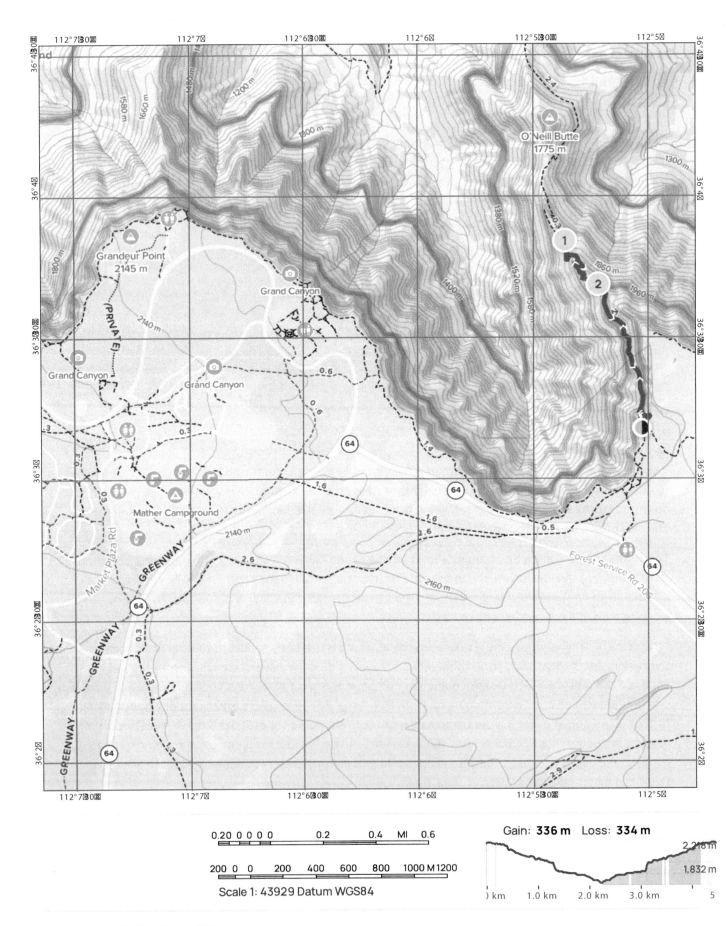

0.20 0 0 0 0   0.2   0.4 MI 0.6

200 0 0   200 400 600 800 1000 M 1200

Scale 1: 43929 Datum WGS84

Gain: **336 m**   Loss: **334 m**

2,218 m

1,832 m

0 km   1.0 km   2.0 km   3.0 km 5

South Kaibab Trail to Cedar Ridge
Grand Canyon, AZ

Start / End
36.05292, -112.08384

South Kaibab Trail to Ooh Aah Point

Head out on this 1.8 miles (2.9-km) out-and-back trail near Grand Canyon, Arizona. Generally considered a moderately challenging route, it takes an average of 1 h 14 min to complete. This is a very popular area for hiking, so you'll likely encounter other people while exploring. The trail is open year-round and is beautiful to visit anytime.

The South Kaibab Trail to Ooh Aah Point hike is one of the easiest hikes around the canyon, but it doesn't compromise at all on views. The views you'll get from the lookout are ones you won't soon forget, so make sure you've got a camera with you to capture the moment.

South Kaibab Trail is one of the best hikes at Grand Canyon South Rim and we personally think it just about has the edge over the more popular Bright Angel Trail. Bright Angel is an amazing trail and you should hike it if you have chance. But South Kaibab has a little more substance to the trail. Views are more open and diverse, the trail itself is more fun and entertaining, and it is a whopping 2.5 miles shorter than Bright Angel to reach Phantom Ranch.

The very first section of descent on South Kaibab as you hike down to Ooh Aah Point is incredibly scenic. Not just views into the canyon, but the trail itself is like something out of a fantasy movie. If you start early enough you will be walking this first section at sunrise and it is something you'll never forget. We were fortunate enough to see booming rays of sun blasting into the canyon as we turned each corner.

The first mile to Ooh Aah Point begins by descending a series of short but steep switchbacks. After the switchbacks, the trail levels out a little and traverses a long promontory into the canyon. The total distance to Ooh-Aah Point, which has a sign, is just under a mile. The mile down is fast and easy, but the hike out takes about twice as long and brings the total distance to around 1.8 miles. If you take it slowly up to the rim, the ascent is not too bad. You will then hug a wall tightly to your right side and it seems that you will never get an open view into the canyon. But you will! And you can tell Ooh Aah Point before you reach the sign marker. That wall to your right ends at the bottom of a staircase and opens up a mind-blowing view.

Many people only hike to Ooh Ahh Point and some will do it for sunrise to get away from the crowds on the Rim.

Tips for Families

1   Hike in the morning. The trail was shaded for most of our hike which was helpful. In the afternoon and evening, this trail will be in full sun.

2   Bring plenty of water. The hike up is tiring and hot.

3   If you want to continue on to Cedar Ridge along this trail, the total distance is 3.0 miles and a total elevation change of 1,120 feet. Many people do this hike, but we were content with Ooh Aah Point.

4   Plan on taking the shuttle. The Yaki Point Road is not open to private vehicles.

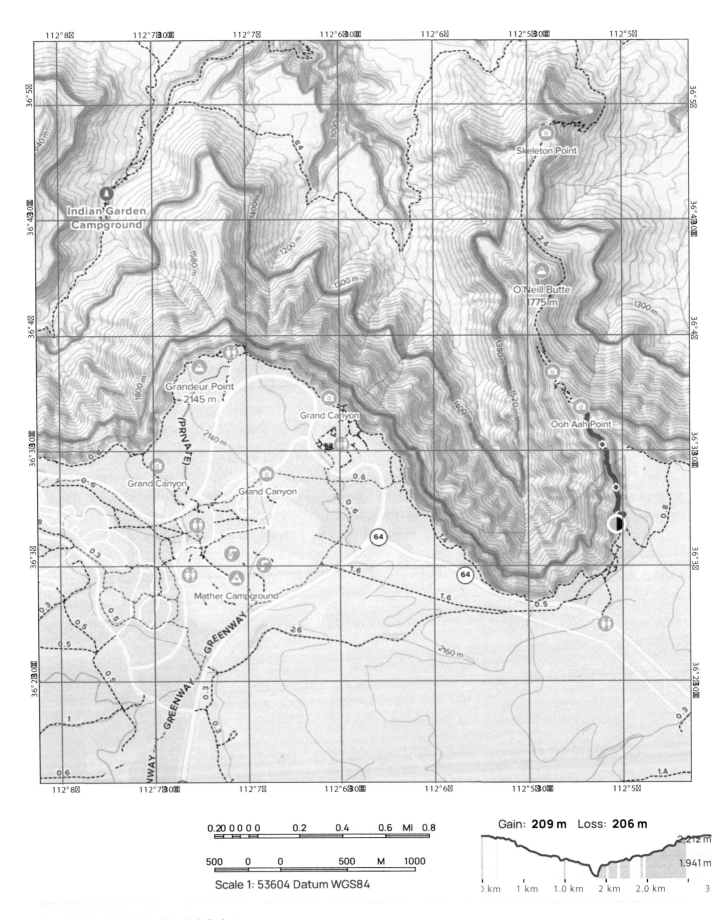

| 112°8⊠ | 112°7⊠30⊠ | 112°7⊠ | 112°6⊠30⊠ | 112°6⊠ | 112°5⊠30⊠ | 112°5⊠ |

Indian Garden Campground

Skeleton Point

O'Neill Butte 1775 m

Grandeur Point 2145 m

(PRIVATE)

Grand Canyon

Grand Canyon

Grand Canyon

Ooh Aah Point

64

64

Mather Campground

GREENWAY

GREENWAY

GREENWAY

0.20 0 0 0 0   0.2   0.4   0.6   MI 0.8

500   0   0   500   M   1000

Scale 1: 53604 Datum WGS84

Gain: **209 m**   Loss: **206 m**

2,212 m

1,941 m

0 km   1 km   1.0 km   2 km   2.0 km   3

South Kaibab Trail to Ooh Aah Point
Grand Canyon, AZ

Start / End
36.05293, -112.08393

Bright Angel Trail

Get to know this 15.3 miles (24.6-km) out-and-back trail near Grand Canyon, Arizona. Generally considered a challenging route, it takes an average of 9 h 6 min to complete. This is a very popular area for backpacking, camping, and hiking, so you'll likely encounter other people while exploring. The best times to visit this trail are October through May.

The South Kaibab and Bright Angel Trails are two of the Grand Canyon's classic hiking trails. You can combine these two trails together to create one massive day hike or a two-day backpacking trip. It is a long, challenging hike but it makes for some incredible memories. With its long distance and nearly a mile of elevation gain, this is a beast of a hike. The Bright Angel Trail begins near the main visitor complex, at the start of the Hermit's Rest Road, and follows the course of Garden Creek, reaching the Colorado after 9.5 miles and a descent of over 4,500 feet. This is the most popular long-distance trail in the national park, and the 'easiest' by which to walk to the river, although most hikers turn back a long way before - one common target is the first of two rest stations after 1.5 miles (the second is after 3 miles), which makes for a round trip of 2 hours or so. The NPS issue stern warnings about the dangers of trying to hike all the way to the river and back in one day, though the journey is quite possible for fit hikers, assuming the weather is not too hot - on some days in midsummer the temperatures of the inner canyon can exceed 110°F, making the trip potentially hazardous. A more reasonable day hike destination is Plateau Point, a viewpoint of the Colorado River, which is reached by a 1.5-mile spur trail for a total trip (one-way) of 6.3 miles.

The Bright Angel Trail is longer than the South Kaibab Trail. But with less elevation gain over a longer distance, it is slightly less strenuous than the South Kaibab Trail. The big advantage of the Bright Angel route over other rim to river paths is that drinking water is available at four locations - the two rest stations, Indian Garden (4.5 miles) and Phantom Ranch at the trail's end - thus mitigating the main danger of Grand Canyon hiking, which is not carrying adequate water. Much of the wide, well used, well maintained but often very dusty trail is along the Garden Creek side canyon so the views are more restricted than on the South Kaibab Trail, which follows a ridge downwards, but the scenery is of course still breathtaking. Rather than hiking, many people opt to travel by mule, which requires reservations many months in advance. Livestock have priority on the trails they use so travelers on foot have to stop and let them pass, and since the mules walk in long convoys and are slow moving as well as quite smelly, they can be rather a nuisance.

As you hike up the Bright Angel Trail, there are several landmarks along the way. Here are their elevations and distances from the Bright Angel Campground.

River Resthouse: 2480 feet, 1.5 miles
Indian Garden: 3800 feet, 4.7 miles
3 Mile Resthouse: 4748 feet, 6.5 miles
Bright Angel Trailhead: 6860 feet, 9.5 miles

Bright Angel Trailhead to Indian Garden- From the River Resthouse to Indian Garden, it is a 3.2-mile walk. The first landmarks are two short tunnels (0.2 and 0.7 miles from the start), taking the path through cliffs of Coconino sandstone. After several more switchbacks, the 1.5-mile resthouse appears - a suitable destination for first time Grand Canyon hikers. This has shade, seating, drinking water and (in season) an NPS ranger in attendance, The next part of the trail becomes gradually more exposed and a little steeper; it crosses a small stream (the upper part of Garden Creek) and descends steadily towards the 3-mile resthouse, which is visible from some distance above. Rather fewer people make it this far, a location 2,100 feet below the rim but less than a third of the way to the trail's end at Phantom Ranch. Past here, following a speedy descent through the Redwall limestone, the route becomes much less steep, and soon starts to move northeastwards, away from the cliffs and along the shallow valley of Garden Creek, where the bushes are mixed with cacti and yucca. After nearly a mile of easy walking, a sign marks the start of Indian Garden - a 1/3-mile-long section of the creek with permanently flowing, spring-fed water that sustains a cool, shady patch of tall cottonwoods and other greenery. In amongst the trees are various buildings, a ranger station, a network of paths, a small herd of deer and the Indian Garden campground, set right next to the creek. Drinking water is available at several places, and an emergency phone.

Indian Garden to the Colorado River- The trail splits at the far side of Indian Garden; right is a continuation of the Bright Angel Trail while left is the Plateau Point/Tonto Trail. The main route continues descending fairly gradually next to the cottonwood tree-lined Garden Creek, crosses a ridge, drops much more steeply into a larger drainage (Pipe Creek) via an exposed series of switchbacks known as the Devils Corkscrew, then continues at stream level one more mile to the Colorado; it next runs alongside the river for a while, traversing the sandy hillside about 50 feet above the water, before crossing the river on a suspension bridge. From here the campsite and lodge at Phantom Ranch are a short walk away up the lower end of Bright Angel Creek, where two other paths branch off: the North Kaibab Trail upstream along the creek, and the Clear Creek Trail to the east.

Plateau Point

The 1.5-mile spur trail to Plateau Point soon moves out of the shade of Indian Garden across a desert-like plateau formed of light brown Tapeats sandstone, covered by sparse grass dotted with occasional barrel cacti and small bushes. The terrain is nearly level, though split by a few shallow gullies, tributaries of Garden Creek to the north. A junction with the Tonto Trail is reached after 0.8 miles, after which the remaining 0.7 miles to Plateau Point is quite straight, ascending slightly to a flat summit then dropping down a little at the far side, past a water tank to a railed viewpoint right at the edge of the Granite Gorge, 1,300 feet directly above the Colorado. About 3 miles of the river are in view, from Bright Angel Canyon to the Horn Creek Rapids; a little more can be seen by walking westwards a way along the rim. The scene is dominated by the dark, rugged igneous cliffs of the inner gorge, formed of Vishnu schist - the oldest rocks in the Grand Canyon. The strata on the far side are tilted, red brown in color but with some brighter red patches of Hakatai shale, the same rocks found most prominently in the lower end of Red Canyon along the New Hance Trail.

The Final Climb - Once you get to 3 Mile Resthouse, appropriately named since it is just 3 miles from the end of the Bright Angel Trail, you are really feeling the climb. By now, you have already started winding your way up the switchbacks. Your thighs are burning, your lungs are burning, and most likely, part of you is wondering why you ever thought that this was going to be a fun thing to do. The final three miles is killer. Take frequent breaks and even though you might not care anymore, try to enjoy the view across the Grand Canyon. Just keep putting one foot in front of the other and eventually you will reach the top of the Bright Angel Trail.

General Description

The Bright Angel trailhead is towards the west side of Grand Canyon Village, right next to the Hermits Rest shuttle stop and immediately west of Kolb Studio. The nearest parking is 1/3 mile away beside the railway tracks at Grand Canyon Station (Lot D). The first 3.5 miles (2,600 feet descent) of the trail are down the cliffs around the side canyon of Garden Creek, so the views remain broadly the same, of the lower end of the creek, the flat land extending to Plateau Point, and Bright Angel Canyon on the North Rim; the landscape does not open out until after Indian Garden, when many more distant cliffs and buttes are visible. The downwards gradient is fairly constant right from the trailhead, descending via numerous long or short switchbacks across bushy hillsides that are in full sun much of the day, though occasional shade is provided by trees or overhanging cliffs. In winter, however, the upper 2 miles are in shadow all day, so the path is likely to be icy. Two sections traverse sheer cliffs (Coconino sandstone and Redwall limestone), while the remainder is across more ledgy, sloping strata of the Hermit, Esplanade and Supai layers. The surface of the trail is formed of bare rock, pebbles or hard-pressed dirt, anchored at intervals by wooden steps, and all (in dry weather) covered in a thick layer of dust caused by the large number of hikers, and the frequent mule trains.

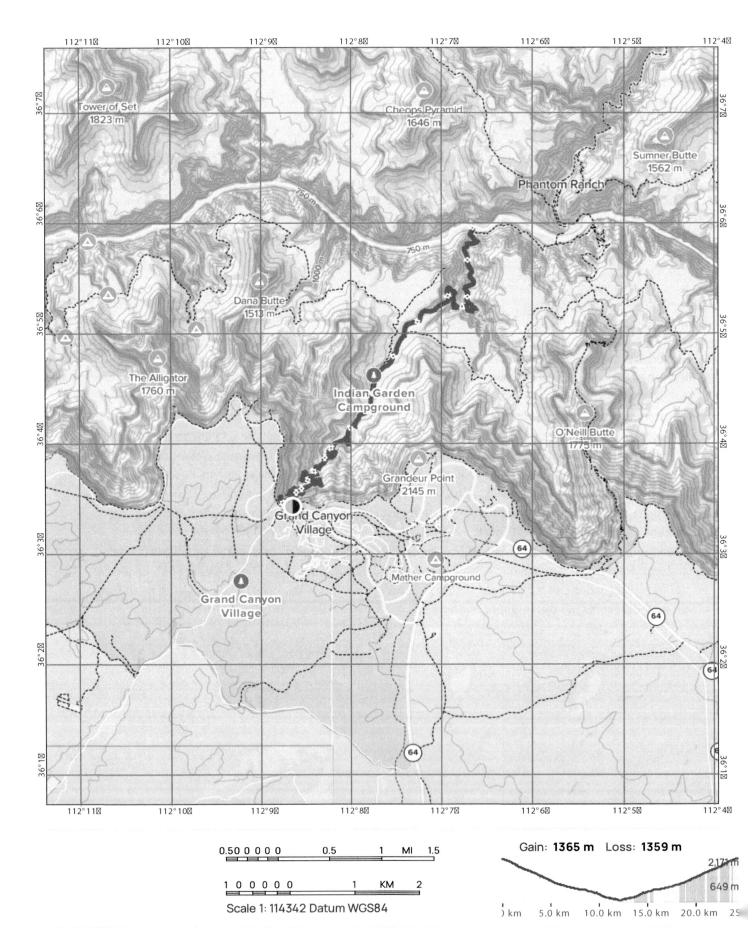

Tower of Set
1823 m

Cheops Pyramid
1646 m

Sumner Butte
1562 m

Phantom Ranch

750 m

750 m

1000 m

Dana Butte
1513 m

The Alligator
1760 m

Indian Garden
Campground

O'Neill Butte
1775 m

Grandeur Point
2145 m

Grand Canyon
Village

64

Mather Campground

Grand Canyon
Village

64

64

64

64

0.50 0 0 0 0   0.5   1   MI   1.5

1 0 0 0 0 0   1   KM   2

Scale 1: 114342 Datum WGS84

Gain: **1365 m**   Loss: **1359 m**

2,171 m

649 m

) km   5.0 km   10.0 km   15.0 km   20.0 km   25

Bright Angel Trail
Grand Canyon, AZ

Start / End
36.05709, -112.14436

Plateau Point via Bright Angel

3 miles Resthouse via Bright Angel

South Kaibab Trail to Skeleton Point

Explore this 5.8 miles (9.3-km) out-and-back trail near Grand Canyon, Arizona. Generally considered a challenging route, it takes an average of 3 h 48 min to complete. This is a very popular area for hiking and horseback riding, so you'll likely encounter other people while exploring.

The South Kaibab Trail is the second-most visited trail in the entire Grand Canyon. With several viewpoints accessible without any extreme hiking, it's a great trail to wander down to take in the grandeur of the Grand Canyon.

Skeleton Point is the furthest you can go on the South Kaibab Trail without navigating extreme terrain, so it's really the best view the average hiker can enjoy before things start to get steep. It's still rated as hard, but when you peer over the edge at the switchbacks below, you'll see what "steep" really looks like in the Grand Canyon! That being said, this route is 1 m wide and the gradient averages at 10%, so it's not exposed or technical.

Skeleton Point shows off the Grand Canyon from the South Rim, which is where most visitors to the canyon go. There may be mules on this trail packing out trash from Phantom Ranch. Should you come up to mules, listen to the handler's directions on how to pass them. If you come up from behind, just announce yourself and listen for instructions on how to pass once it's safe to do so.
The trailhead isn't accessible by private vehicle, so you'll need to take the orange shuttle or the hiker's express shuttle. There's a lot just east of Yaki Point Road that you can use to access the trailhead as well.

From the trailhead, you'll hike out along the ridge. About a half-mile into the outbound trip, you'll pass Yaki Point on your right, a popular viewpoint. At the point, look out over the amazing view to the east. Ahead of you is Cedar Ridge, a popular turnaround point for casual hikers.

Ahead of Cedar Ridge is O'Neill Butte, from which there's plenty of canyon to appreciate in almost all directions. Hiking around the east side of the butte, you'll continue the last few steps to Skeleton Point. Look out at Buddha Temple, Isis Temple, The Colonnade, and Brahma Temple across the Colorado River.

Once you're ready to head back, you'll simply retrace your steps back to the trailhead and either walk back to where you parked or take the shuttle back.

Once you're done, consider a stop into the Yavapai Museum of Geology on the South Rim to learn more about the fascinating geological history of the canyon.

When to Hike

There are many important personal factors that affect your timing (work, partner schedules, finances, etc.), we won't be speaking to those but we will provide guidance on timing as it relates to weather and crowds.

The Grand Canyon itself influences the weather. Temperature and precipitation vary greatly due to the canyon's stark elevation changes. For every 1,000 feet that you descend into the canyon towards the Colorado River, the air temperature increases another 5.5 degrees Fahrenheit. As such, you can expect Skeleton Point to be at least 11F warmer than at the trailhead.

Remember, the South Rim is well over 7,000' above sea level. It often gets very cold and icy in the winter and early spring. Additionally, while Skeleton Point might not receive frozen precipitation, the South Rim and a good portion of the trail could be snowy or icy. This can sometimes accumulate to the point you would need micro-spikes and trekking poles or even have to reschedule your adventure due to road closures.

On the other end of the spectrum, summer gets incredibly hot, especially on the exposed canyon trails. The lack of shade and rising temperatures increases the risk of experiencing heat exhaustion if you're not properly prepared. According to the National Park Service, hikers are rescued from the canyon every day during the summer. If your personal factors don't allow you the luxury of skipping out on these extreme weather swings, be prepared and enjoy the journey as safely as possible.

For the winter, you'll want to stay on top of the weather at the rim, check road conditions, and have the appropriate gear (micro-spikes, trekking poles, insulating layers, water, etc.). For the summer, you'll want to start your journey as early as possible (at or before sunrise, if possible), bring plenty of water, and eat salty snacks. Preparing properly for both extremes doesn't mean that you'll be 100% free of unexpected challenges, so take your time and turn around if you don't feel confident in the current circumstances.

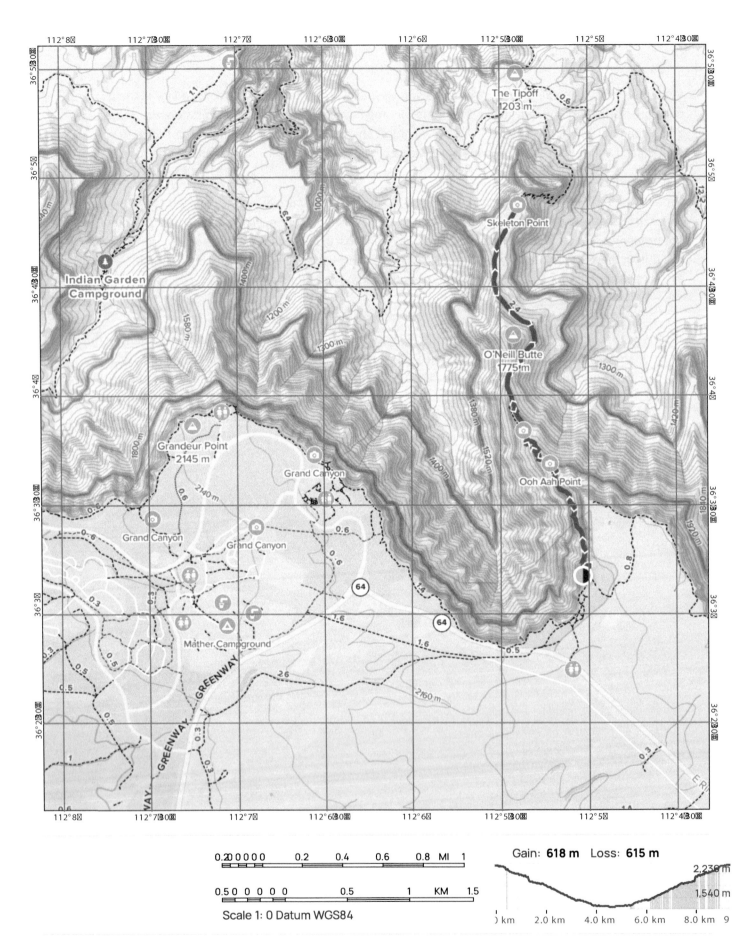

0.2 0 0 0 0 0   0.2   0.4   0.6   0.8   MI   1

0.5 0 0 0 0 0   0.5   1   KM   1.5

Scale 1: 0 Datum WGS84

Gain: **618 m**   Loss: **615 m**

2,238 m

1,540 m

0 km   2.0 km   4.0 km   6.0 km   8.0 km   9

South Kaibab Trail to Skeleton Point
Grand Canyon, AZ

Start / End
36.05285, -112.08392

Grand Canyon Rim: Mules to Mather Point

Get to know this 6.0 miles (9.7-km) out-and-back trail near Grand Canyon, Arizona. Generally considered an easy route, it takes an average of 2 h 8 min to complete. This is a very popular area for walking, so you'll likely encounter other people while exploring. The trail is open year-round and is beautiful to visit anytime.

This is a less popular easy route located near Grand Canyon Village Arizona. This hike primary route can be used both directions and has an easy overall physical rating. This route climbs 108 m with a max elevation of 2,172 m then descends -108 m.

The entire Rim Trail stretches from the South Kaibab Trailhead west to Hermit's Rest and is approximately 13 miles long. The trail is mostly paved and lined with markers to show you how far you've traveled both in feet and years (an earth timeline if you will). Very fun for kids and educational too. Mather Point is the closest Grand Canyon overlook to the visitor's center. While you can walk this section in under an hour it is recommended to plan for a longer trip as you'll want to take your time to appreciate all the good views, snag a few pictures, and experience the Trail of Time, which overlaps this section of the rim. The 2-mile (3.5 km) section between Yavapai Geology Museum and the Grand Canyon Historic Village can be hot and sunny in the summer time so be sure to take water, snacks, and sun protection. Water and restrooms are available at the Geology Museum, Grand Canyon Visitor and at multiple spots in the village. This section of the trail is quite popular as well, but offers more opportunities for solitude and quiet moments along the canyon's edge. When the Village (Blue) Route shuttle bus is running transportation will run between the Grand Canyon Visitor Center and the Village to help complete a one-way loop. Dogs are allowed on-leash on the Rim Trail but not on the shuttle busses so plan accordingly.

Accessibility:

There are at least 10 designated accessible spaces in the paved parking lot off of South Entrance Road at the east end of the trail. All of them are van-accessible with striped access aisles. There are wheelchair accessible shuttle stops close to the trail and parking lots along the trail to access it at different points. The trail surface is paved asphalt and smooth. It is typically at least 5 feet wide. The most accessible portion of the trail is the first about 1.3 miles when going west. The majority of the trail is estimated to be in the mostly gentle (5% or less) grade category but there are steeper sections at about 1.3-1.4, 1.9, 2.5, and 2.7 when going west. Trail goers using wheelchairs/mobility equipment or strollers may need assistance in the steeper sections or to avoid them for safety. The trail may be slippery due to snow in the winter or thunderstorms in the summer so use caution.

Getting there

Directions from South Entrance Station: Drive 3 miles north to Grand Canyon Village. The visitor center lies in this cluster of buildings.

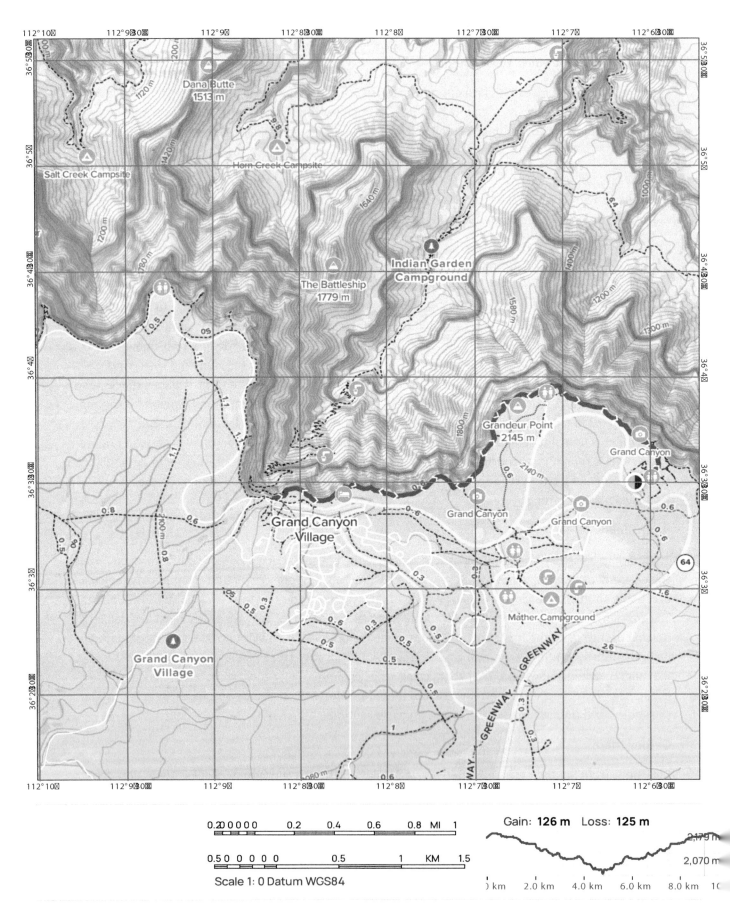

| 0.20 0 0 0 0 | 0.2 | 0.4 | 0.6 | 0.8 | MI 1 |

| 0.50 0 0 0 0 | 0.5 | 1 | KM 1.5 |

Scale 1: 0 Datum WGS84

Gain: **126 m**   Loss: **125 m**

2,179 m

2,070 m

0 km   2.0 km   4.0 km   6.0 km   8.0 km   10

Grand Canyon Rim: Mules to Mather Point
Grand Canyon, AZ

Start / End
36.05832, -112.10986

Shoshone Point Trail

Check out this 2.1 miles (3.4-km) out-and-back trail near Grand Canyon, Arizona. Generally considered an easy route, it takes an average of 45 min to complete. This is a very popular area for birding, hiking, and running, so you'll likely encounter other people while exploring. The best times to visit this trail are May through November.

Hidden just a mile off the South Rim Road, this easy hike to Shoshone Point is worth your while. The Shoshone Point Trail is a beautiful walk through a Ponderosa Pine Forest to a serene picnic spot, and then to a hidden rock formation and Shoshone Point. If you want to get away from the crowds of tourists stopping at the roadside attractions, this short hike is for you.

Accessibility: Visitors using wheelchairs, mobility equipment, or strollers may need all-terrain tires or adaptive/motorized equipment for the surface type and grade. Visitors using wheelchairs, mobility equipment, or strollers may need assistance in the steeper sections or to avoid them for safety. The most accessible portion of the trail is the first about 0.1 miles.

Accessible Parking:

Parking lot surface: gravel;

There do not appear to be any designated accessible parking spaces within 1.0 miles of the trailhead.

Trail Details:

Trail surface: a natural surface (dirt, rocks, roots);

Average trail width: 5 feet;

Estimated average grade category: mostly gentle (5% or less) with steeper sections at about 0.2 and 0.9-1.0 miles when going northeast;

Picnic tables: yes, picnic tables at the north end of the route.

The Shoshone Point Trail starts at a gate and unsigned parking pullout just west of mile marker 246 on Desert View Drive. The quiet trail is a nearly level dirt road that gains only 100 feet over its mile length. Cross the plateau hiking through a wooded area covered with ponderosa pine. After a mile, emerge at the turn around a loop where there are benches, grills, mule hitching posts and pit toilets. The covered pavilion can be rented for events, but you don't need a permit just to visit the overlook.

The views of the eastern Grand Canyon area from the rim here are great, but thrill seekers press on to the very edge of Shoshone Point. Be careful with the loose rock and narrow ledges, a fall would be deadly. Check out the cool mushroom/headstone rock formation at the point. See if you can identify Hance Rapids, Desert View Tower, Vishnu Temple, Horseshoe Mesa and many other landmarks. Enjoy the solitude of this unpopulated gem, then retrace your steps back to the parking area. This is also a popular place to watch the sunset (bring a headlamp for the hike back).

Waypoints

1 First view 36.04323, -112.05922   **2 Travis's Rock** 36.03677, -112.06579

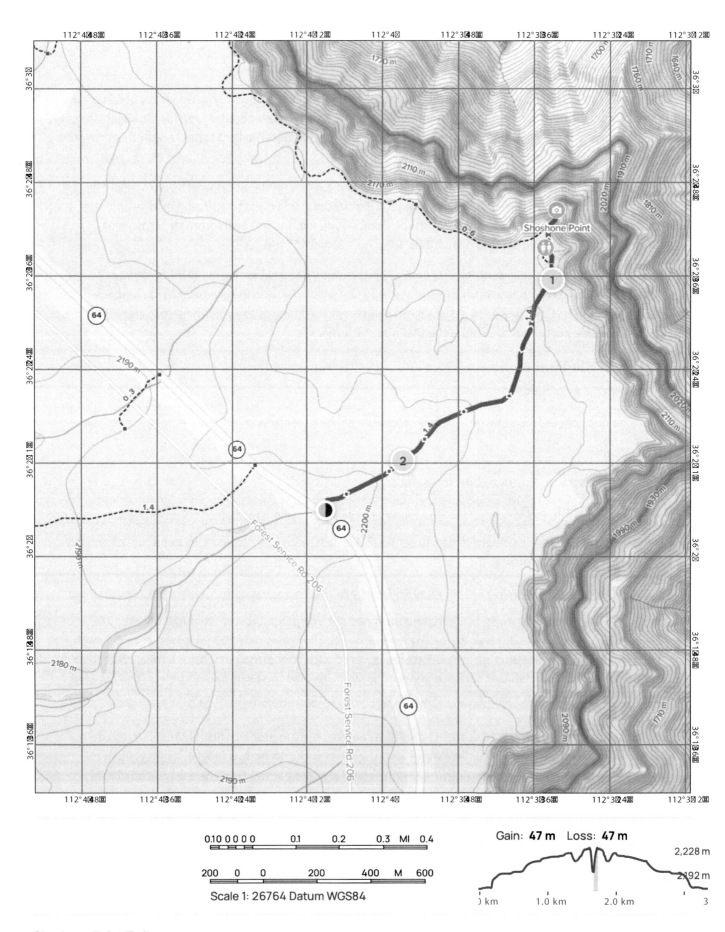

1770 m
1700 m
1710 m
1640 m
1760 m
2110 m
2170 m
1910 m
1810 m
2020 m
Shoshone Point
0.6
1.4
64
2190 m
0.3
64
1.4
2200 m
64
2110 m
2020 m
1990 m
1930 m
Forest Service Rd 206
2190 m
1710 m
2090 m
2180 m
Forest Service Rd 206
2190 m
64

36°3' 36°2'48" 36°2'36" 36°2'24" 36°2'12" 36°2' 36°1'48" 36°1'36"

0.10 0 0 0 0   0.1   0.2   0.3   MI   0.4

200   0   0   200   400   M   600

Scale 1: 26764 Datum WGS84

Gain: **47 m**   Loss: **47 m**

2,228 m

2,192 m

0 km   1.0 km   2.0 km   3

Shoshone Point Trail
Grand Canyon, AZ

Start / End
36.03497, -112.06922

Yavapai Point via Rim Trail

Explore this 1.6 miles (2.6-km) out-and-back trail near Grand Canyon, Arizona. Generally considered an easy route, it takes an average of 32 min to complete. This is a very popular area for walking, so you'll likely encounter other people while exploring.

The Rim Trail follows a large stretch of the South Rim of the Grand Canyon, where most visitors to the park end up making their home base. Yavapai Point is one of the popular viewpoints on the South Rim, and the ease of access to this trail and this viewpoint make both extremely popular with visitors.

If you come to the Grand Canyon, you'll likely end up walking on the Rim Trail without even meaning to. It's the main route that links each of the many viewpoints over the canyon, and it's a very laid-back trip. All ages and skill levels can enjoy this walk.

The route begins from the Grand Canyon Village, so you can stop into the Visitor Center to learn about the canyon and get your day's activities planned before heading out, or you can grab a snack or drink to take along. Since this route originates from the village, there's no need to figure out the shuttle system to enjoy it.

The Rim Trail can be used to reach the trailheads at Yavapai Point for hikers bound for longer trips since Yavapai Point offers extremely limited public parking. You can also use this route as a warm-up for longer trips on the South Kaibab Trail or Bright Angel Trail. Or, just wander along to soak up the expansive view as far as you like before heading back.

This route begins near Mather Point, one of the main viewpoints on the South Rim. You'll hike left (west) along the trail that hugs the rim. There are viewpoints dotted all along the trail, so stop frequently to absorb the sheer size of the geological anomaly before you.

The route continues to Yavapai Point, where an interesting geology museum is worth a stop if you're interested in how the canyon was formed. The museum is equally fun for kids and adults, with interactive exhibits providing a thorough explanation of how the canyon came to be.

From Yavapai Point, you'll turn around and retrace your steps to the main village. Should you not wish to walk back, you can catch the orange shuttle back to the village instead.

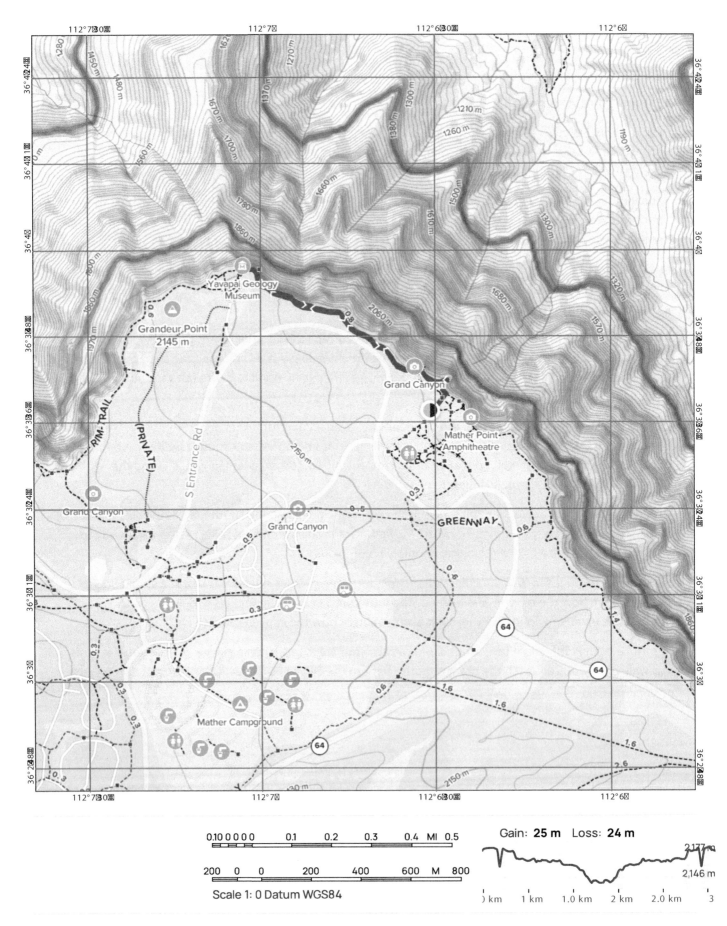

Yavapai Geology Museum

Grandeur Point
2145 m

RIM TRAIL

(PRIVATE)

S Entrance Rd

Grand Canyon

Grand Canyon

Grand Canyon

Mather Point
Amphitheatre

GREENWAY

64

64

64

Mather Campground

0.10 0 0 0 0   0.1   0.2   0.3   0.4   MI   0.5

200   0   0   200   400   600   M   800

Scale 1: 0 Datum WGS84

Gain: **25 m**   Loss: **24 m**

2,177 m
2,146 m

0 km   1 km   1.0 km   2 km   2.0 km   3

Yavapai Point via Rim Trail
Williams, AZ

Start / End
36.06045, -112.10861

South Kaibab Trail to Tip Off

Discover this 8.9 miles (14.3-km) out-and-back trail near Grand Canyon, Arizona. Generally considered a challenging route, it takes an average of 5 h 59 min to complete. This is a popular trail for backpacking, birding, and hiking, but you can still enjoy some solitude during quieter times of day.

The South Kaibab Trail is the second-most visited trail in the entire Grand Canyon. With several viewpoints accessible without any extreme hiking, it's a great trail to wander down to take in the grandeur of the Grand Canyon. This route is possible to complete in a day for fit hikers, but you can also opt to turn this into a backpacking trip by continuing further to Phantom Ranch on South Kaibab Trail.

There may be mules on this trail packing out trash from Phantom Ranch. Should you come up to mules, listen to the handler's directions on how to pass them. If you come up from behind, just announce yourself and listen for instructions on how to pass once it's safe to do so.

From the trailhead, you'll hike out along the ridge. About a 0.5 mile into the outbound trip, you'll pass Yaki Point on your right, a popular viewpoint. At the point, look out over the amazing view to the east. Ahead of you is Cedar Ridge, a popular turnaround point for casual hikers. Ahead of Cedar Ridge is O'Neill Butte, from which there's plenty of canyon to appreciate in almost all directions. Hiking around the east side of the butte, you'll continue to Skeleton Point. This is where things get interesting.

Descend through very steep switchbacks, arriving at the Tip Off just past the restrooms. Take a moment to take in the view here and rest up before the steep hike back to the trailhead.

Waypoint

1

Tip Off Point - Grand Canyon

36.0916, -112.08917

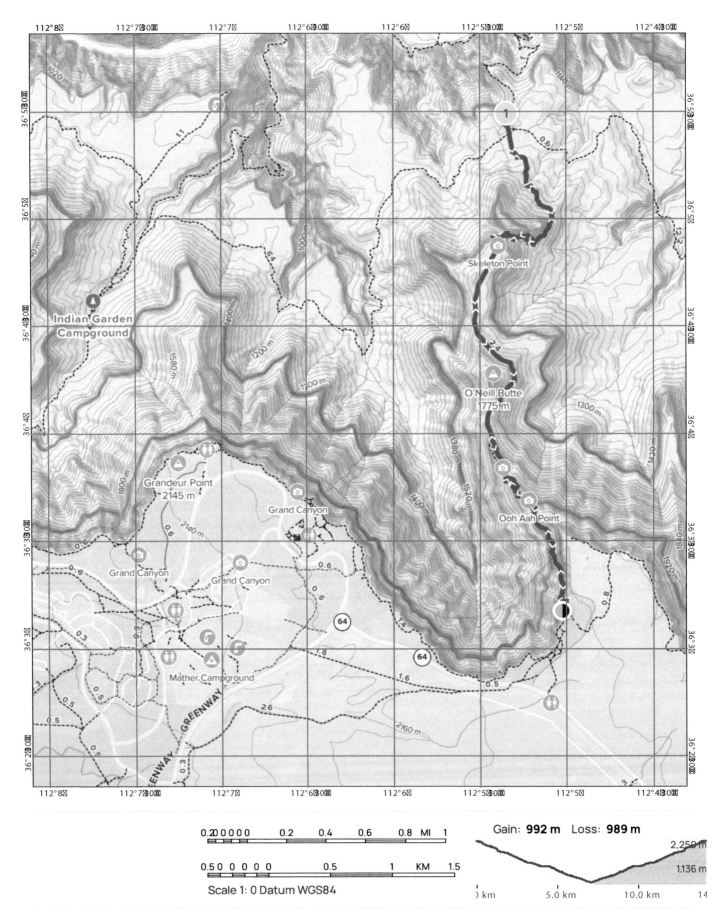

112°8℗	112°7℗30℗	112°7℗	112°6℗30℗	112°6℗	112°5℗30℗	112°5℗	112°4℗30℗		

Skeleton Point

Indian Garden
Campground

O'Neill Butte
1775 m

Grandeur Point
2145 m

Grand Canyon

Grand Canyon

Grand Canyon

Ooh Aah Point

64

64

Mather Campground

GREENWAY

GREENWAY

0.2 0 0 0 0 0   0.2   0.4   0.6   0.8   MI   1

0.5 0 0 0 0 0   0.5   1   KM   1.5

Scale 1: 0 Datum WGS84

Gain: **992 m**   Loss: **989 m**

2,250 m

1,136 m

0 km   5.0 km   10.0 km   14

South Kaibab Trail to Tip Off
Grand Canyon, AZ

Start / End
36.05285, -112.0838

Grandview Point to Horseshoe Mesa Trail

This is a 5.7 miles (9.2-km) out-and-back trail near Grand Canyon, Arizona. Generally considered a challenging route, it takes an average of 4 h 18 min to complete. This is a very popular area for hiking, so you'll likely encounter other people while exploring.

Easily the toughest and most rugged of the Grand Canyon Park Service's recommended day hikes, the Grandview Trail to Horseshoe Mesa is not for the faint of heart. The trail was built in 1893 by miners, and after a few minutes on the Grandview, you'll realize that people were a lot tougher back then. The route is an engineering marvel, with steep cobbled sections and wood cribs hugging the cliffside that lead down to an abandoned mine site at Horseshoe Mesa. This day hike offers expansive views, natural beauty, and a break from the Grand Canyon crowds.

The trail has panoramic views of Sinking Ship, Coronado Butte, Krishna Shrine, Wotans Throne, and much more. Set in a less busy part of the South Rim, this route provides the chance to test your hiking chops Grand Canyon style without needing to contend with as many fellow hikers as Bright Angel or South Kaibab require. This out and back approach is easier and shorter than the Grandview Trail Loop, which encircles Horseshoe Mesa.

This is a hard hike with some intimidating sections. Those who are afraid of heights may want to choose another route. There is only one spring to refill your water at and you'll be out in the sun nearly the whole way. Lots of water, snacks, good boots, and poles are helpful.

The route heads out from Grandview Point along the Coconino Saddle towards Horseshoe Mesa. This saddle is very exposed with steep dropoffs, so hike carefully and watch your step. Once you make it to the mesa, you'll pass the campsite and end your route where the route splits. Check out the view in every direction around you before retracing your steps back to the trailhead.

Getting there

The Grandview Trail is located at Grandview Point, about a 15-minute drive east from the Grand Canyon Visitor Center (South Rim). The trailhead at Grandview Point is at the scenic overlook; expect lots of tourists. But it's far enough away from the main South Rim attractions that there's almost always parking at the trailhead area

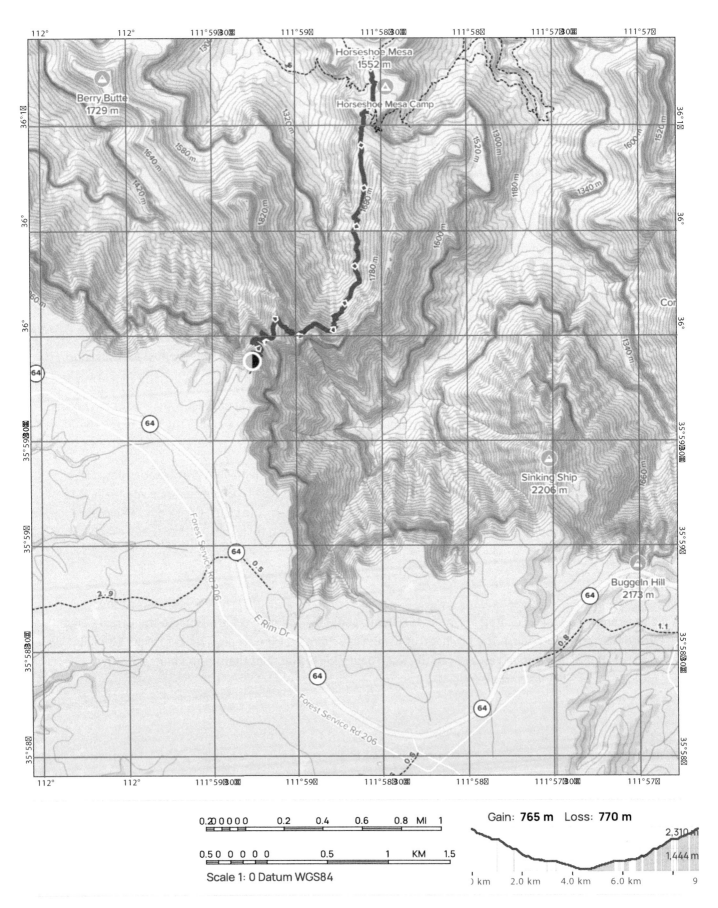

112°	112°	111°59'30"	111°59'	111°58'30" 111°58' 111°57'30" 111°57'

Horseshoe Mesa
1552 m

Horseshoe Mesa Camp

Berry Butte
1729 m

Sinking Ship
2206 m

Buggeln Hill
2173 m

Forest Service Rd 206

E Rim Dr

Forest Service Rd 206

0.20 0 0 0 0   0.2   0.4   0.6   0.8   MI   1

0.5 0   0   0   0   0   0.5   1   KM   1.5

Scale 1: 0 Datum WGS84

Gain: 765 m   Loss: 770 m

2,310 m

1,444 m

0 km   2.0 km   4.0 km   6.0 km   9

Grandview Point to Horseshoe Mesa Trail
Grand Canyon, AZ

Start / End
35.99796, -111.98779

Roaring Springs via North Kaibab Trail

This is a 11 miles (17.7-km) out-and-back trail near North Rim, Arizona. Generally considered a challenging route, it takes an average of 6 h 53 min to complete. The best times to visit this trail are March through October.

The North Rim of the Grand Canyon is a less-visited gem for hikers who want all the scenery with far lighter crowds. This quieter side of the canyon is home to a hike that definitely competes when it comes to the best day hikes in the Grand Canyon. The hike to Roaring Springs on North Kaibab Trail leads you through unforgettable scenery as you scale down the wall of this mighty canyon.

You'll pass breathtaking viewpoints, hike through tall tunnels blasted into the rock, and dip your feet in the cooling springs that emerge from the lush canyon walls. It's a scenic, varied trek that's especially nice on a warm day when you can cool your feet in the springs.

There is one water station on this trail, but we still recommend bringing a large reservoir to help with the steep ascent. Poles and good boots will be helpful, and you should prepare for the varied weather at the North Rim. It can be very hot in the summer and very snowy in the winter.

If hiking all the way to the spring is too much for your group, you can take this trail to the Coconino Overlook, which is less than a mile down.

From the trailhead, you'll descend down into Bright Angel Canyon. Three-quarters of a mile in, stop at the Coconino Overlook to look down into the Roaring Springs Canyon. From here, it's on to the Supai tunnel, where there's a water station and rest stop.

The tunnel is quite interesting, with a passageway blasted right through the thick pink limestone. Continue along a sometimes tree-lined and sometimes open trail as it switchbacks through the rocks. This set of switchbacks is out in the sun, so you'll want to have a full water bottle before heading down.

5.5 km in, cross the Redwall Footbridge to get to the west side of the canyon. Peer over the edge to take in the massive canyon. Past the bridge, you'll hike a dizzying narrow ridge along the canyon wall. This trail was also blasted out of the rock, and it's quite amazing.

Hike through more switchbacks, after which you'll start to hear the springs. The waterfall flows down the cliff, flanked by green shrubbery. A quick side trail takes you to the springs, the perfect spot to rest awhile.

Mules have played an integral part in creating and maintaining these trails. Even before the completion of the North Kaibab Trail in 1928, mule teams have been used to haul supplies and people from rim to rim. If you'd like a ride down the trail on a mule, find more information at the visitor center or at the trailhead.

Overall, this is a highly recommended trail! The North Rim as a whole is a must-see if you find yourself in Arizona. They have beautiful cabins you can stay in for as low as $143/night.

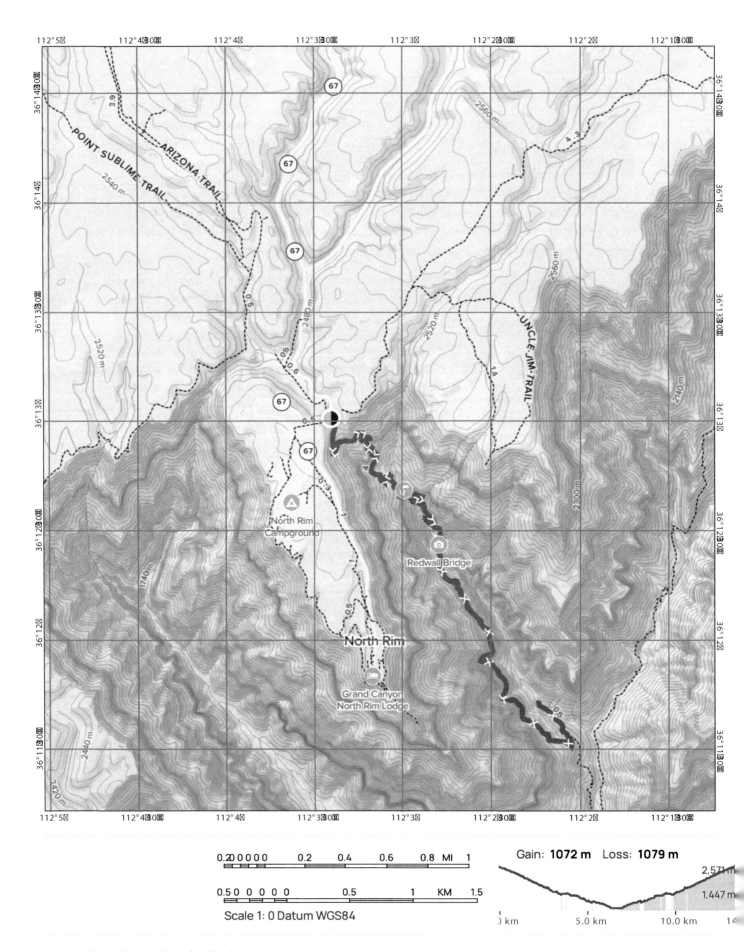

112°5′ 112°4′30″ 112°4′ 112°3′30″ 112°3′ 112°2′30″ 112°2′ 112°1′30″

36°14′30″ 36°14′ 36°13′30″ 36°13′ 36°12′30″ 36°12′ 36°11′30″

POINT SUBLIME TRAIL

ARIZONA TRAIL

UNCLE JIM TRAIL

67

North Rim Campground

Redwall Bridge

North Rim

Grand Canyon North Rim Lodge

0.20000 0.2 0.4 0.6 0.8 MI 1

0.50000 0.5 1 KM 1.5

Scale 1: 0 Datum WGS84

Gain: **1072 m**   Loss: **1079 m**

2,571 m

1,447 m

0 km   5.0 km   10.0 km   14

North Kaibab Trail to Roaring Springs
Fredonia, AZ

Start / End
36.21687, -112.05678

Transept Trail

This is a 2.9 miles (4.7-km) out-and-back trail near North Rim, Arizona. Generally considered a moderately challenging route, it takes an average of 1 h 7 min to complete. This is a popular trail for birding, hiking, and walking, but you can still enjoy some solitude during quieter times of day. The best times to visit this trail are May through October.

The road to Grand Canyon's North Rim ends at Bright Angel Point beside Grand Canyon Lodge, from where most people, on first arriving, make the short walk south to the main canyon viewpoint, a place usually very busy. A more peaceful encounter with this part of the gorge, albeit lacking such far reaching views, is provided by the easy, mostly level Transept Trail which follows the canyon rim from the lodge to the North Rim Campground, 1.5 miles away.

The path runs through mixed pine, oak and aspen woodland along the edge of The Transept, a deep but relatively short tributary of the much longer Bright Angel Canyon; it also provides a backdrop for the first few miles of the even less traveled Widforss Trail. Some parts of the Transept Trail wind through quite dense woodland, out of sight of the canyon, but most is right by the edge, so giving good views across the Transept, and of more distant cliffs and ravines to the south. The route is fairly well used, a bit dusty in places, semi-shaded and not at all difficult.

The path begins directly below Grand Canyon Lodge, in view of those sunbathing on the open-air terrace next to the cafe, from where it heads north, passes a railing-protected viewpoint then runs beneath a row of log cabins. These comprise just a few of the 200 rooms available at the lodge, but are some of the most desirable as they have partial canyon views though the pine trees. Next, the trail moves away from the rim for a short distance, to avoid a short side canyon, before climbing back to the edge of the Transept, and following it northwards. Several narrow spur paths snake through the bushes to the very edge of the cliffs, and one promontory about half way along projects out rather more so has the best view of all. A little off-trail scrambling is necessary for the best panorama. From here the path curves around another small ravine then turns away from the rim, ascending slightly to the North Rim Campground. A loop hike can be made by returning via the 1.2-mile Bridle Trail, a not-so-interesting path (also a cycle route) that parallels the main road back south.

The Transept is particularly steep on the far (west) side, where sheer cliffs of the Coconino, Supai and Redwall layers fall 2,500 feet almost vertically down, and form part of a straight ridge extending south as far as Oza Butte, beyond which the land drops away at the edge of Bright Angel Canyon. The middle third of this canyon can be seen from the Transept Trail, including three prominent peaks on the far rim - Deva Temple, Brahma Temple and Zoroaster Temple. Several miles beyond are Grandview and Shoshone Points on the South Rim, and, on the horizon, the volcanic cone of Red Butte.

Getting there

Directions from North Rim Entrance Station: Drive southward along North Rim Parkway Hwy 67 to the end. Take the outside back steps just outside the Grand Canyon Lodge (North Rim) dining room to the trailhead and head north. Trailhead is just above the visitor overlook. You can also reach the trail from the Transept / North Rim campground, as the trail connects the campground to the lodge.

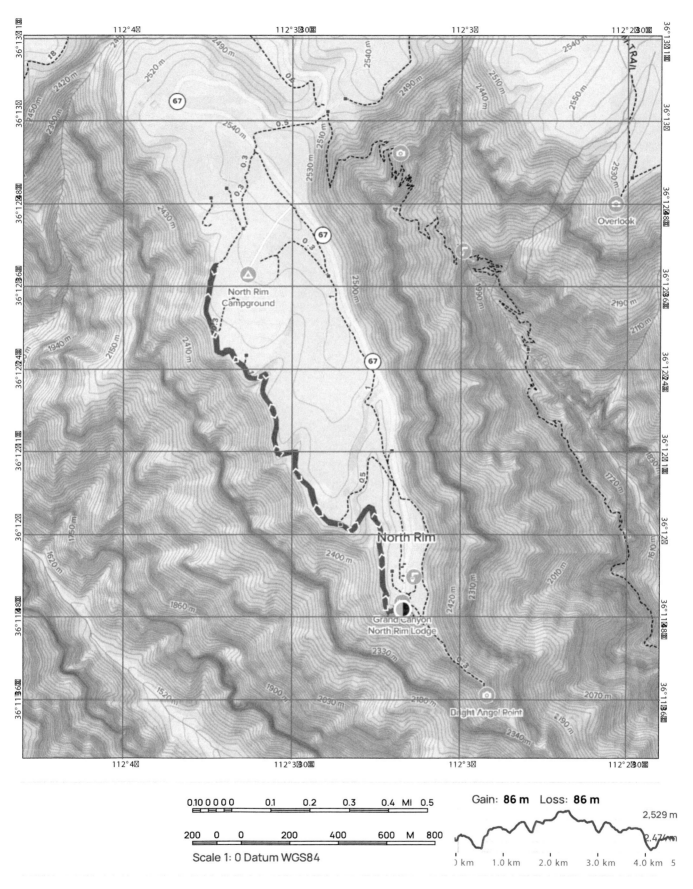

Gain: **86 m**   Loss: **86 m**

2,529 m

2,47 m

0 km   1.0 km   2.0 km   3.0 km   4.0 km   5

0.10 0 0 0 0   0.1   0.2   0.3   0.4 MI 0.5

200   0   0   200   400   600 M 800

Scale 1: 0 Datum WGS84

Transept Trail
Fredonia, AZ

Start / End
36.19695, -112.05287

Widforss Trail

Experience this 9.3 miles (15.0-km) out-and-back trail near Grand Canyon, Arizona. Generally considered a moderately challenging route, it takes an average of 3 h 47 min to complete. This is a very popular area for backpacking, hiking, and running, so you'll likely encounter other people while exploring. The best times to visit this trail are May through October.

The trail is named after Gunnar Widforss, an early twentieth-century artist from Sweden. He lived and painted at the Grand Canyon in the 1930s, producing a large collection of watercolors prized for their geologic detail. Widforss tried to capture the Grand Canyon environment as he saw it then. That environment has changed over the years as natural and human forces continue to reshape a picture characterized by monumental change through the eons.

Like most footpaths on the North Rim of the Grand Canyon, the Widforss Trail runs across the plateau rather than descending over the edge, passing close to the side of a deep, red-walled ravine (The Transept) for the first half then turning away through the forest before emerging into the open near Widforss Point. A large area of buttes and side canyons can be seen from this final overlook, centered on Haunted Canyon, a narrow tributary of Phantom Creek, although the views to the east are blocked by a thin promontory extending a little way further south. This is Widforss Point, beyond the end of the trail but accessible with quite a lot of effort by scrambling half a mile across a steep, overgrown ravine.

The route to the main viewpoint is shaded and mostly level so not particularly challenging, though very pleasant; even the section through the woods, out of sight of any canyons, is scenic and enjoyable. Some might find the high elevation (around 8,000 feet) makes the walk more tiring that might otherwise be expected.

The trail begins a little way along the unpaved track leading to Point Sublime, branching off the North Rim entrance road shortly before the main visitor complex, and just back from the much more frequented North Kaibab Trailhead. The track crosses a secluded grassy clearing in the forest (Harvey Meadow), often surrounded by melting snow drifts well into June, before reaching the Widforss parking area; past here, the surface becomes rougher as the road continues east for many miles towards several remote overlooks, also including Bedivere Point, Tiyo Point and Swamp Point. The first half of the Widforss Trail, as far as The Transept, is described in an NPS brochure (25¢) available at the trailhead, describing 14 numbered points of interest.

In the first half of the Transept, the path is level for a way, across part of the meadow, before starting to climb a hillside into shady, mixed forest of pine, spruce, aspen, maple and fir. It winds in and out of a small ravine, the first of six such minor diversions, then approaches the canyon rim for the first time, allowing fleeting views of the tall Kaibab, Coconino and Redwall cliffs around the upper end of The Transept. As is the case for most overlooks along the trail, the views are always slightly obscured by trees - there is no sheer drop-off like at many South Rim viewpoints, just a marked steepening of the slope, so the tops of trees further down the hillside are in the line of sight. But the scenery does become gradually better and less obstructed as the path moves further west. The best vistas are between stops 11 to 13 (2 miles), near the far side of The Transept, from where all of the deep gorge is in view, and part of the larger Bright Angel Canyon in the distance. The high cliffs at either side block much sight of the main Grand Canyon, however.

In the second half after the last numbered sign, the path turns away from the rim and descends a shallow valley, passing through light, airy woodland showing signs of recent wildfire damage. The edge of the canyon comes briefly close once more before the trail climbs to the top of a low plateau, completely surrounded by ponderosa pine and aspen forest, now rather more burnt by the fire. The place is peaceful, especially on clear, warm, windless mornings - conditions that often prevail in early summer. Wildflowers grow profusely in the sunny ground between the tree stumps, colorful birds flutter about, and larger animals like deer, coyote and the distinctive Kaibab squirrel may be glimpsed. The pure white bark and effervescent green leaves of the aspen trees as ever look especially striking against a deep blue sky.

The path ends at a picnic area with table and chairs, in a clearing in the trees just before the land falls away steeply at the edge of the canyon. This tranquil spot has fine views south and partly west, though not east as that direction is hidden by the ridge leading to Widforss Point, a slightly higher and more isolated summit about half a mile away, separated from the end of the trail by a bushy ravine - the very upper end of Haunted Canyon, which is the main drainage to the south. This canyon is bordered by a narrow ridge at each side - on the left rise the prominent buttes of Manu Temple & Buddha Temple, and on the right is the wider span of The Colonnade, with Isis Temple further away and the cliffs of the South Rim beyond that, 9 miles distant. Widforss Point offers even better views, but the off-trail walk across a ravine filled with spiky bushes and up the steep limestone hillside beyond is rather difficult. Trail and point are named after Gunnar Widforss, a landscape artist who painted many scenes at the Grand Canyon early in the 20th century.

Getting there

Directions from North Entrance Station: Drive southward on North Rim Parkway to an intersection. The road to the left leads to the North Kaibab Trailhead. The road to the right follows a dirt road one mile to the Widforss Trailhead.

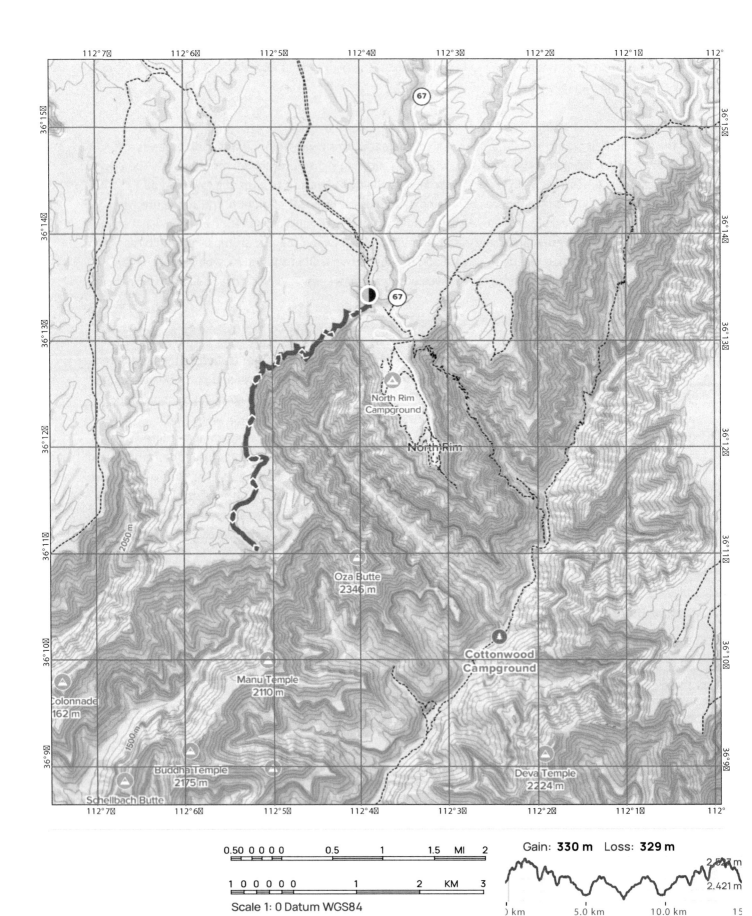

| 112°7⊠ | 112°6⊠ | 112°5⊠ | 112°4⊠ | 112°3⊠ | 112°2⊠ | 112°1⊠ | 112° |

67

67

North Rim
Campground

North Rim

Oza Butte
2346 m

Cottonwood
Campground

Manu Temple
2110 m

Colonnade
162 m

Buddha Temple
2175 m

Deva Temple
2224 m

Schellbach Butte

2050 m

1500 m

| 0.50 0 0 0 0 | 0.5 | 1 | 1.5 | MI | 2 |

| 1 0 0 0 0 0 | 1 | 2 | KM | 3 |

Scale 1: 0 Datum WGS84

Gain: **330 m**   Loss: **329 m**

2.527 m

2.421 m

) km   5.0 km   10.0 km   15

Widforss Trail
Fredonia, AZ

Start / End
36.22372, -112.065

Cape Final Trail

This is a 4 mile (6.4-km) out-and-back trail near North Rim, Arizona. Generally considered an easy route, it takes an average of 1 h 39 min to complete. This is a popular trail for camping and hiking, but you can still enjoy some solitude during quieter times of day. The best times to visit this trail are May through October.

Like nearby Cape Royal, Cape Final offers almost a 270° panorama over the eastern Grand Canyon, with the advantage that the viewpoint is less obscured by trees; all the scene is viewable from a single spot, so this is perhaps the best of the north rim overlooks. The point may be reached by a two-mile hike on an old forest track, long since closed to all vehicles, and although the walk is easy and mostly level, few people make the trip hence the viewpoint has the added benefit of solitude. Quite a small parking area is provided at the trailhead, which is located in a clearing in the tall pine woods 2.5 miles north of the road's end at Cape Royal.

From the carpark, the route climbs gently, curving through the woodland up to a flattish area that offers very pleasant walking - the surface is flat and free of stones, the gradient gentle, and the surroundings shady. The trees are well separated, and the forest floor has no undergrowth so the views are quite extensive even though the trail affords no immediate glimpse of the canyon rim. Some parts of the forest show signs of recent wildfires. The path descends into a shallow basin and veers north, approaching the plateau edge for the first time, and giving a vista of red buttes and cliffs around the upper end of Lava Creek, before turning back south, away from the rim. The final section runs through more open woodland of smaller trees, down a slope, through a cluster of bushes and up between a few large boulders to the point.

The main difference between Cape Final and other viewpoints further west is that the cliffs on the far side of the Colorado rise up almost vertically from the river to the rim, with hardly any tributary canyons - two great, colorful escarpments (Desert Facade and Palisades of the Desert) together extend for 20 miles, broken only by the narrow gorge of the Little Colorado River, one of the largest tributaries of the Grand Canyon. The actual confluence is not in view, as it is hidden behind two buttes of Kaibab limestone (Chuar and Temple), which became infamous in 1956 as the site of a plane crash resulting from a mid-air collision, an accident that caused the deaths of 128 people. The land between here and Cape Final has the usual mixture of mesas, cliffs and ravines, with the most prominent features in the foreground being Juno Temple, Jupiter Temple, Unkar Creek and Freya Castle. Several miles of the south rim plateau are in view, while the eastern horizon is formed by the even flatter Painted Desert, part of the Navajo Indian Reservation, where the elevation change is less than 100 feet over a 12-mile stretch of the rim.

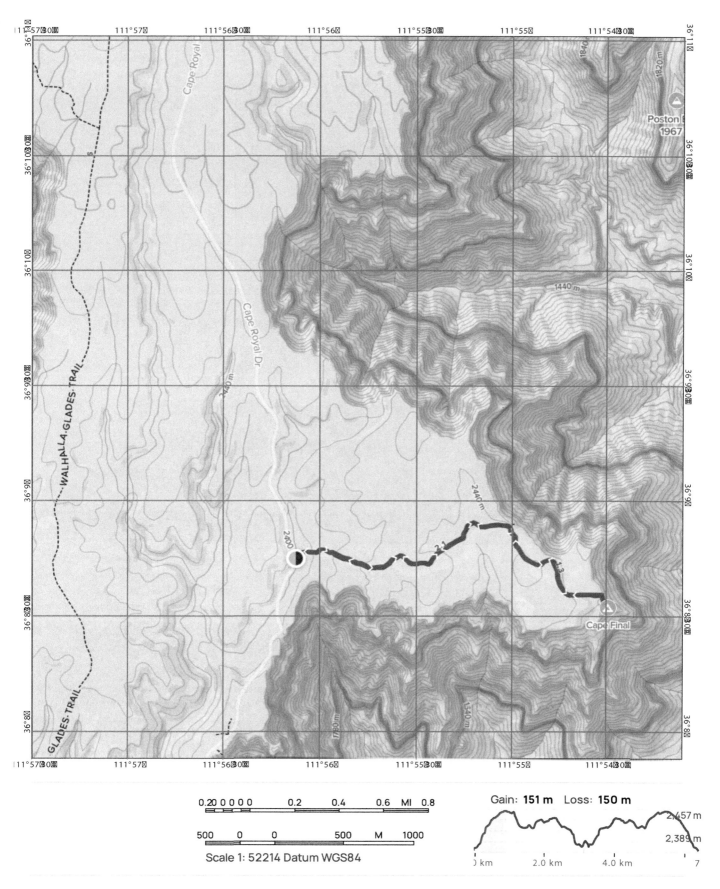

0.20 0 0 0 0   0.2   0.4   0.6 MI 0.8

500   0   0   500   M 1000

Scale 1: 52214 Datum WGS84

Gain: **151 m** Loss: **150 m**

2,457 m

2,389 m

0 km   2.0 km   4.0 km   7

Cape Final Trail
Fredonia, AZ

Start / End
36.14579, -111.9355

Hopi Point Trail

This is a 3.8 miles (6.1-km) out-and-back trail near Grand Canyon, Arizona. Generally considered a moderately challenging route, it takes an average of 1 h 29 min to complete.

Stop number four along the west rim shuttlebus (the red route) is Hopi Point, From the trailhead, hike away from the village on West Rim Trail as it runs alongside Hermit Road. The route then pulls away from the road to follow the rim as it begins to reach north. You can stop into the Trailview Overlook for a midway viewpoint when it comes up on your right.

You'll now be hiking between the rim and Hermit Road again. You'll pass Maricopa Point as the route turns west, so feel free to take a quick detour here to enjoy the view. The route passes by Powell Point next, the last viewpoint before Hopi Point.

Hugging the rim, you'll arrive at Hopi Point. Dana Butte rises right ahead of you, The Battleship on your right, and The Alligator on your left. The Colorado River snakes below these formations.

Snap photos and take it all in. If you're lucky enough to be here when not many others are, you can listen to how still and quiet the air is over this massive marvel.

Once you're ready, you'll return to the village on the same route you used to hike out. Alternatively, you can keep hiking on the Rim Trail to check out more viewpoints further west.

This is the northernmost spot on this part of the south rim, and the first point where much more of the western Grand Canyon comes into full perspective - another 20 miles, since the Colorado begins a big bend northward, allowing views all the way to Havasupai Point and the Great Scenic Divide. Hopi Point has a fenced viewing area next to the road, and a vista over the canyon centered on Dana Butte, a flat mesa 2,000 feet below the overlook. Salt Creek runs to one side, meeting the Colorado at a series of rapids, while Monument Creek is on the other side, joining the river at another set (Granite Rapids).

Opposite Hopi Point on the North Rim are a group of prominent mesas either side of Trinity Creek, named after figures from ancient Egypt - largest are Isis Temple, Horus Temple and Osiris Temple. Like many other Grand Canyon features their names were assigned by writer and geologist Clarence Dutton in the 1880s.

Because of the wide-ranging, unobstructed views, Hopi is the most popular place on the west rim for watching the sun set.

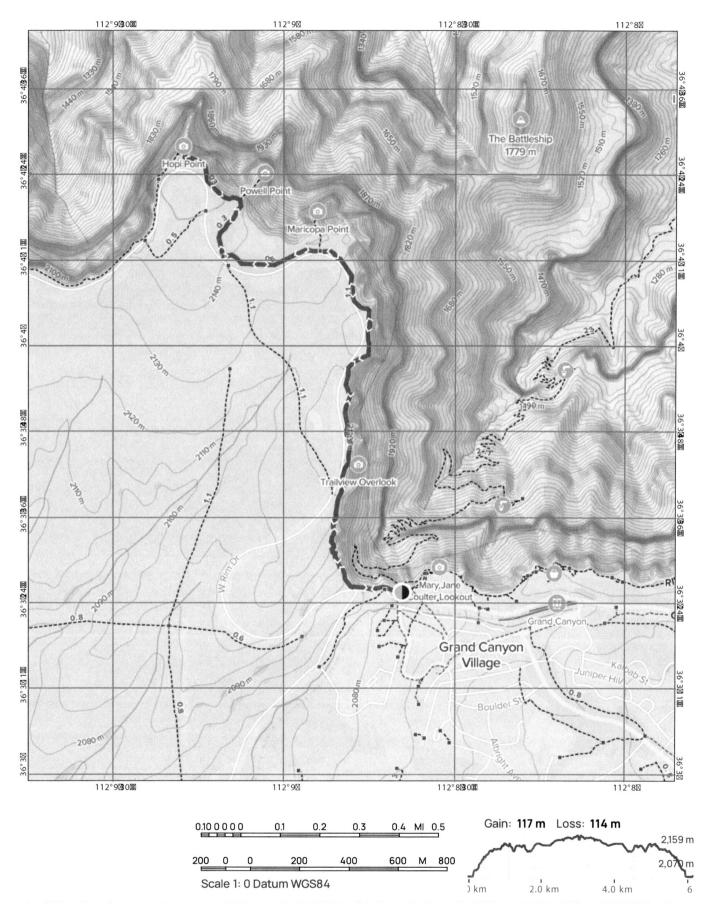

Gain: **117 m** Loss: **114 m**

2,159 m

2,070 m

0 km   2.0 km   4.0 km   6

0.10 0 0 0 0   0.1   0.2   0.3   0.4 MI 0.5

200   0   0   200   400   600 M 800

Scale 1: 0 Datum WGS84

Hopi Point Trail
Grand Canyon, AZ

Start / End
36.05705, -112.14429

Printed in Great Britain
by Amazon

34772628R10051